THE
QUEEN MOTHER

THE
QUEEN
MOTHER

Helene McGowan

Grange

Published by Grange Books
An imprint of Books & Toys Ltd
The Grange
Grange Yard
London SE1 3AG

Produced by
Bison Books Ltd
Kimbolton House
117A Fulham Road
London SW3 6RL

ISBN 1-85627-018-1

Printed in Hong Kong

10 9 8 7 6 5 4 3 2 1

CONTENTS

PROGRESS TOWARDS ROYALTY

The Queen Mother was born Lady Elizabeth Bowes-Lyon, somewhere in London on August 4 1900. Her exact place of birth is not known but it is definitely not the village of St Paul's Walden Bury in Hertfordshire (her childhood family home), which mistakenly appears on her birth certificate. What is certain is that she was christened there, in the village church, Lady Elizabeth Angela Marguerite Bowes-Lyon on September 23 1900.

The family 'seat' was Glamis Castle in Scotland, 12 miles north of Dundee and set in the Grampian hills. Proud possessor of a fine and ancient tradition, the castle has belonged to the Strathmore family since 1372, and dates back to the eleventh century. It is believed that Mary Queen of Scots was entertained there and the story persists that William Shakespeare visited there shortly before writing *Macbeth*, in which King Duncan is slain by the Thane of Glamis (happily not an ancestor of the Strathmore family). One famous King who is an ancestor of the Queen Mother's is Robert the Bruce of Scotland; an honor she shares with King George VI.

LEFT The Queen Mother (or Lady Elizabeth Bowes-Lyon as she then was), photographed at Glamis Castle as a young woman.

RIGHT Lady Elizabeth aged eight, in a watercolour by Mabel Hankey.

8

LEFT The 'Two Benjamins' as their mother affectionately called Elizabeth and her younger brother David, with their dancing master.

ABOVE Lady Elizabeth and Princess Mary (Bertie's younger sister). Princess Mary's wedding to the Earl of Harewood was Elizabeth's first taste of a major Royal event.

BELOW Elizabeth receives a bouquet in March 1923, just one month before she becomes Duchess of York.

There were ten children altogether in the happy, friendly, country family that provided such perfect beginnings for the little girl who would one day be Queen of England. Her parents were happily married and brought up their children to share their steadfast moral values, unsnobbish attitudes and religious faith. Her mother Cecilia, Countess of Strathmore, was an easy-going, vivacious, artistic and musical woman who was devoted to her children and they to her. Many who knew them both feel the Queen Mother shares her mother's strength of character and warm, charming personality. Lady Strathmore's favourite saying was, 'Life is for living and working at'. With the help of her modest, devout and dutiful husband she provided a disciplined, encouraging and very loving family atmosphere in which her children could thrive.

As the photographs from those early years show, Elizabeth was a very beautiful child with a mass of dark curls and china-blue eyes. Lord Gorrel, when he was a Secretary of State in Lloyd George's government (1916-22), wrote in praise of her that she was 'as responsive as a harp, wistful and appealing one moment, bright-eyed and eager the next . . . quick of intelligence, alive with humour . . . touchingly, and sometimes amusingly, loyal to her friends'. Her nursemaid Clara (who many years later looked after the young Princesses Elizabeth and Margaret), also remembered her as a delightful child: 'She was an easy-going, happy baby, running at 13 months and speaking very young'.

Like all aristocratic families of the day, the Strathmores moved home several times a year. They spent the social season in their London house at 20 St James' Square, holidays at Glamis and the rest of the year at St Pauls, Walden Bury. They also owned a fourth home – Streatham Castle in County Durham. Of all her siblings Elizabeth was closest in age to David, who was born two years after her in 1902. They were also close to each other in temperament and remained devoted to one another until David's death in 1972. Just as she is now a country woman at heart, so she was then a country child. She very much enjoyed the country pursuits of haymaking, collecting eggs from the pet bantam hens, and gathering wild strawberries in the summer. She loved to invent new outdoor games with her brother David, and to work in her own little garden plot. There were always plenty of things to do, ranging from playing tennis or croquet to having fun with the family pets which included the pigs Emma and Lucifer, kittens, puppies, tortoises and her pony Babs.

Elizabeth was educated by governesses. Her idyllic, sunny home life was only interrupted very briefly when she attended a select academy for young ladies in South

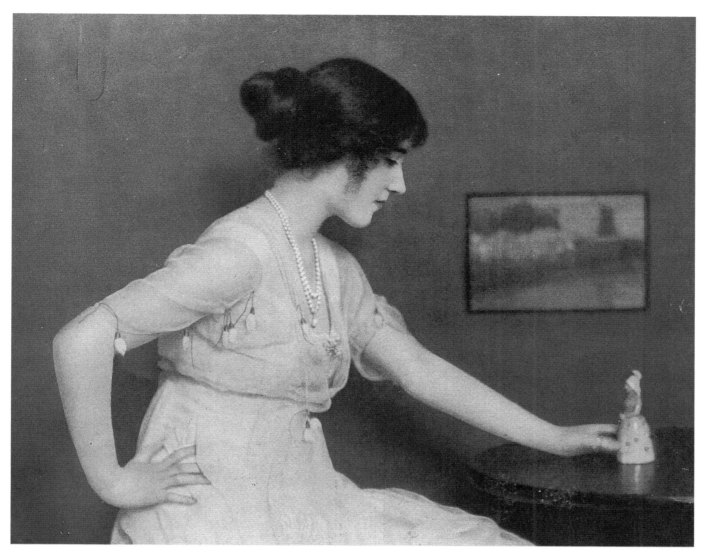

LEFT A formal study of Elizabeth.

BELOW LEFT The handsome young Duke of York.

LEFT This study by society photographer Van Dyke shows the young Elizabeth's delicate beauty.

Kensington, where she won an essay prize. It was on August 4 1914 that Elizabeth's life did change abruptly, when World War One broke out on her fourteenth birthday. The Strathmore family quickly became embroiled in this 'war to end all wars'. Glamis Castle was turned into a military hospital where soldiers from the Dundee Royal Infirmary were sent to convalesce. The war years saw Elizabeth mature from a charming girl into a responsible, wise young woman. She came to know the injured soldiers by name and generally made herself invaluable to all around her. She did all she could to cheer up the patients, many of whom were lonely and homesick and only a few years older than herself. She wrote their letters home, played cards and billiards with them, and played piano as they sang along (a favourite song was 'Goodbye Dolly, I must leave you').

Tragically, her brother Fergus was killed in action at Loos in 1915. He had served with the Black Watch, as did all the Strathmore brothers. It was one of several regiments of which, as Queen, Elizabeth was to become Colonel-in-Chief. His death brought her even more responsibility as her mother struggled to cope with her loss. The family was also informed that another brother, Michael, had been killed, but little David Bowes-Lyon refused to believe this, insisting that he was only injured. Happily, this insight proved true for the family were soon told the true facts – Michael had been severely wounded in the head and taken prisoner of war. One of the fifteen thousand soldiers who spent time recuperating at Glamis during the war remembered the teenage Elizabeth with gratitude and affection: 'We were all amazed; for her fifteen years she was very kind hearted, womanly and most sympathetic'.

The war ended in November 1918, and it was not long before the parties began. Elizabeth became a much sought after 'deb'; her old-fashioned prettiness and gracious charm set her apart from the cocktail-drinking, chain-smoking girls who were more typical of Polite Society in the early 1920s. Lady Burton, a friend of her mother's, wrote in a letter: 'Elizabeth Lyon is out now, and Cecilia has had a party for her. How many hearts Elizabeth will break'. She did indeed make conquests and one of these was a shy, gauche young man known as Bertie, or more formally Prince Albert, second son of King George V. It is often stated that the two met for the first time at a dance given by Lady Farquhar on May 20 1920. In fact this was their second encounter, for they had met as children at the birthday party of a mutual friend; the five-year-old Elizabeth had sweetly presented ten-year-old Bertie with the cherries from the top of her cake.

The moment he saw her dancing with his equerry James Stuart, Bertie was seriously smitten and promptly claimed the next dance. He was already a friend and shooting companion of her brothers and Elizabeth was well acquainted with Bertie's younger sister Princess Mary, whom she had met through her connection with the Girl Guide Movement. Bertie began to visit Glamis much more often, and in the autumn of 1919 Elizabeth showed him round the castle she loved so much. According to his mother Queen Mary, Bertie could now talk of little else but Elizabeth whose 'radiant vitality' had entirely captivated him. The warm, relaxed atmosphere of Glamis Castle, continually filled with the sound of music and laughter, could not help but impress the young Prince who was used to the rigid, very formal way of life at Buckingham Palace.

When he informed his father of his desire to marry Elizabeth, the King replied in typically forthright manner: 'You'll be a lucky feller if she accepts you'. Bertie had to wait a while for his luck for Elizabeth refused several proposals before finally accepting him. She felt torn between her desire to make Bertie happy and her doubts about taking on the responsibilities of a royal marriage. She knew she had not been prepared from childhood and was worried that she could not cope with the stresses and strains of such a public role. The Prince's sadness and dejection were obvious to everyone. Lady Strathmore had become very fond of her daughter's persistent suitor and expressed her sympathy for him when she said: 'I like him so much, and he is a man who will be made or marred by his wife'. Queen Mary was thinking very much along the same lines. She saw Elizabeth as 'the only girl who could make Bertie happy'.

On February 28 1922, Elizabeth was a bridesmaid at the wedding of Princess Mary to the Earl of Harewood. She very much enjoyed this major royal event, and throughout the rest of the year she and Bertie grew closer and closer. His shyness and lack of confidence slowly dissolved as his love for her grew. For her part, she found it hard to resist his honesty, affection, modesty and obvious goodness. On January 13 1923 she accepted him as they were walking in the woods at St Paul's Walden Bury. The Prince sent a telegram in pre-arranged code to his parents: 'All right, Bertie'. He wrote to his mother that he knew he was 'very lucky' to have won Elizabeth over at last. It was soon announced that the wedding would take place on Thursday, April 20 1923, in Westminster Abbey. On hearing the news Chips Channon, the American social commentator, wrote in his diary: 'There is not a single man in England who does not envy him. The clubs are all in gloom'.

The man that Elizabeth had chosen to marry was born on December 14 1895. Unfortunately this date was also the anniversary of the death of Prince Albert, much to the horror of Albert's widow and the baby's great grandmother, Queen Victoria. As a consolation to her the child was christened Albert but was always known by friends and family as Bertie. He had not had the privilege of the kind of blissful childhood his fiancée had enjoyed. He was a quiet, introverted and withdrawn child who had the misfortune to suffer from knock-knees and a stammer. The latter ailment was not tackled successfully until he was in his thirties but he did undergo a cure for his misshaped knees as a child, which involved being stuck for six months in painful splints. A further blight to his childhood years was his unstable nursemaid, who fed him unsuitable nursery food, leading to a lifetime of gastric complaints. He was naturally lefthanded but was forced to write with his right hand, which may have been partly responsible for his stammer.

Like his brothers and sisters, Bertie found his father's teasing difficult to cope with and as a child was rather afraid of him. His older brother, the confident, handsome and devastatingly charming Prince Edward, always seemed to outshine him. His sterling qualities were there, however, for anyone who cared to look closely enough. When Bertie went to Naval School at thirteen, his tutor wrote of him: 'I have always found him a very straightforward and honorable boy'. He grew up to be goodlooking and a fine athlete, despite his health problems, competing in the Wimbledon Tennis mens' doubles in 1926 with his friend Louis Greig. In World War One he served in the Navy and, though dogged with ill health, the experience gave him new confidence. On board *HMS Collingwood* he witnessed the Battle of Jutland in 1916, and as a reward for his war efforts his father awarded him the Order of the Garter. He was very disappointed when poor health forced him out of the Navy after the war. He spent a term studying Economics at Trinity College, Cambridge, and while he was there he began his work in industrial welfare and social reform. The Duke of York's camps were set up to bring together boys from working class homes and public schools. This was a highly innovative idea at the time, and the Prince's genuine interest and concern for the problems of the young people helped by the schemes impressed everyone involved. Bertie had been created Duke of York in 1920 by his father in recognition of his sense

TOP The King and Queen, President and Madame Poincaré of France, the Prince of Wales, Sir Douglas Haig, and Sir Francois Bertle in July 1917.

ABOVE Before the wedding, 26 April 1923.

RIGHT ABOVE Queen Mary leaving a St John's Ambulance Brigade Hospital in 1917.

RIGHT BELOW The Duke of York and his new bride Elizabeth, Duchess of York, returning from Westminster Abbey.

of duty and hard work. In a letter to his son the King allowed himself a few affectionate words: 'I feel this splendid old title will be safe in your hands.'

Clouds were gathering in the sky as the wedding day dawned, and it was raining when Elizabeth entered the Abbey on the arm of her father. But when she emerged a royal bride, the sky was bursting with sunshine. The couple spent their honeymoon at Polesden Lacey, a beautiful, spacious house in secluded Surrey countryside, and at Glamis. The Scottish weather was appalling during their stay and Elizabeth succumbed to whooping cough – not a very romantic illness, as she lamented to a friend. Elizabeth was now the fourth lady in the land after Queen Mary, Princess Mary and the Princess Royal (the King's sister). Everyone, not least the King and Queen, were delighted with the match; as the King wrote to his second son: 'You are indeed a lucky man to have such a charming and delightful wife as Elizabeth and I am sure you will both be very happy together'.

THE UNWELCOME THRONE

T he Yorks were given White Lodge as their marital home. It was in a very romantic setting in Richmond Park, with wild deer roaming round, but was too big and much too far from London. However, it was Queen Mary's childhood home and it was her dearest wish that the Yorks make it their home. The new Duchess soon made herself an integral member of the 'family firm'. She was a tremendous help and support to her husband but always took care not to upstage him. She nurtured and encouraged in him the qualities which, by the time of his death, would be known throughout the world. She helped to increase his fragile self-confidence and his faith in himself. Queen Mary pronounced her a 'great addition to the family', and King George could not even bring himself to criticize her occasional lateness, a fault he normally abhorred in anyone. Instead he confided to the Archbishop of Canterbury that if she were not sometimes late, 'she would be perfect'.

The Royal Family was greatly in need of a pretty, charming, young woman to help

FAR LEFT Sir Gerald Kelly's formal portrait of Queen Elizabeth in her coronation gown.

LEFT This delightful photograph of the Duchess of York with her two daughters and their pets was taken just six months before the Abdication Crisis.

ABOVE A portrait of the new Duchess of York, painted in 1924 by R G Eves.

with the hard work and incessant tours that were so necessary if the British monarchy was to survive where so many of its European counterparts, not to mention relations, had foundered. During an official visit to Northern Ireland the Duchess's instinctive knowledge of how to endear herself to a crowd and smile her way through public occasions became evident for the first time. The Duke gave voice to his admiration for her: 'I am very lucky indeed to have her to help me. She knows exactly what to do and say to all the people we meet'. At home, the Yorks led a quiet and very contented life. They would read, listen to music recitals, visit friends, and the Duke would do his favorite hobby – his needlework.

In 1924 the Yorks embarked on a once in a lifetime adventure, a private trip to East Africa. They left England on December 1 1924 for a four-month holiday which involved roughing it in tents and very long foot safaris. The Duke's considerable prowess at shooting bagged him two rhinos, two lions and two buffaloes. They journeyed through Kenya and Uganda, and saw the White Nile and the Red Sea. When they returned home via the Sudan the Duke felt relaxed and in great health. He was even happier when the Duchess presented him with the news that she was expecting a baby in the following spring. They were now living in the Strathmore family home at 17 Bruton Street while their new home at 145 Piccadilly was being renovated and decorated for them. It was at Bruton Street that Princess Elizabeth was born at 3.40 am on April 21 1926. She was christened Elizabeth Alexandra Mary (the same initials as her mother) on May 29 in the private chapel at Buckingham Palace.

The Duchess was very much a working mother. She gradually took on more and more responsibilities and royal duties. She became patron of several hospitals, including St Mary's Paddington where many years later several of her grandchildren were to be born. In 1927 she became Colonel-in-Chief of her first regiment, the King's Own Yorkshire Light Infantry. It was the first of many. In the same year she was made Burgess of the City of Glasgow, and Commander-in-Chief of the St John's Ambulance Brigade the following year. She and the Duke were very happy, just as the King and many others had predicted. But there remained one stumbling block to their lives as public figures and this was the Duke's stammer, which was still very evident. The problem became even more pressing when they learned that the Duke would have to

OPPOSITE Just one of the many official duties of the Duke and Duchess of York: visiting the Wembley Exhibition, May 1925.

LEFT A Duchess for only three months, Elizabeth's relaxed Royal style is already in evidence as she and her husband attend the Fresh Air Fund Outing in July 1923.

BELOW Yet another bouquet for the very fashionably attired Elizabeth as she and the Duke of York pay an official visit to Ilford in October 1926.

18

open the Commonwealth Parliament in Canberra as part of the forthcoming tour of Australia and New Zealand. The Duchess decided to persuade her husband to make one last attempt to cure the stammer.

Appropriately enough, they chose an Australian speech therapist called Lionel Logue to treat the Duke. The Duchess accompanied her husband on some of the weekly visits to Logue's consulting rooms and helped Bertie practise the breathing exercises that were an essential part of the treatment. Their joint efforts worked; several months later the stammer was very much improved. His fear of public speaking greatly relieved, the Duke and Duchess prepared for the first major tour of their marriage. They were very sad to leave eight-month old Elizabeth behind but, despite the suffering and tears the parting involved, the Yorks put their sense of duty first.

They sailed from Portsmouth on January 6 1927. It was a rough voyage and a very tough initiation into naval travel for the Duchess. The tour was the first of many triumphs for her in the Common-wealth. Their ship the *Reknown* took a leisurely route, stopping off at Tenerife, Panama and Jamaica before finally reaching New Zealand on February 22. The tour was especially important for the Yorks as it was the first time either of them had undertaken such a major royal visit. The New Zealanders made sure their guests felt very welcome. The crowds were always overjoyed to see the

ABOVE The Duchess became Colonel-in-Chief of the King's Own Yorkshire Light Infantry in 1927. Here she is visiting the regiment for the first time at Aldershot in December 1927.

RIGHT The Yorks were delighted when their first daughter Elizabeth was born in April 1926. This picture shows the Duchess leaving 17 Bruton St for the christening at Buckingham Palace.

20

royal couple and everywhere they were presented with gifts for little Princess Elizabeth. Unfortunately, when they reached the South Island the Duchess fell ill with tonsillitis and a raging temperature. The Duke was convinced that the massive crowds that had turned out to see both of them in Wellington would not be repeated now he was by himself. With his wife's encouragement he went on alone, however, and was pleasantly surprised when he received a rapturous reception in Christchurch. With the Duchess well again, they set sail for Australia where they visited New South Wales, Queensland, Tasmania, Victoria and then Canberra where, although very nervous, the Duke managed to make a successful speech for the opening of the Commonwealth Parliament.

They arrived home on June 27 1927 and were welcomed back by the Prince of Wales and the King and Queen. There was a joyful reunion between Princess Elizabeth (now fourteen months old), and her parents. The success of the tour endeared them even further to the King, who also adored his little granddaughter. Sadly his relationship with Edward, the Prince of Wales, was deteriorating rapidly. A steward at Buckingham Palace overheard an exasperated King say to his eldest son: 'You dress like a cad, you act like a cad, Goddamit you are a cad. Get out.' One of King George V's last wishes was to prove prophetic: 'I hope that my son never marries and has children, and that nothing comes between Bertie, Lillibet and the throne'.

The Yorks had not long been happily ensconced in their new home at 145 Piccadilly when the Duchess announced she was expecting another child. The Duke was very pleased for he had wanted to complete their little family for some time. Princess Margaret was born on a stormy night at Glamis Castle on August 21 1890. She was the first royal child to be born in Scotland since the mid-seventeenth century. The King was so happy at having another granddaughter that he gave her parents the Royal Lodge Windsor as a present; it became a very special private weekend home, where the Yorks spent many happy hours designing the lovely gardens. Margaret's arrival only emphasized further that Prince Edward was still showing no signs of settling down. Everyone assumed it was only a matter of time before he married and provided an heir to the throne. As we all now know so well, they were to be proved very wrong.

Wallis Simpson arrived on the scene in 1934 and soon became the latest in a long line of companions to the Prince of Wales when she replaced Thelma, Lady Furness and Mrs Freda Dudley Ward in his affections. She had come to England a few years earlier with her husband Ernest Simpson. This simple event precipitated a major constitutional crisis. The Duchess of York met Mrs Simpson but was never to feel relaxed in her company. Understandably, she has always found it hard to forgive her for the

ABOVE This portrait of Elizabeth dressed in 1920s high fashion reveals why she so captivated Bertie when they first met as adults in 1922.

RIGHT The Queen Mother has long been renowned for her common touch and skill at putting others at their ease. Here she is shaking hands with an ex-service member of the British Legion in Weston-super-Mare in July 1928.

ABOVE The Duke and Duchess of York are greeted by cheering crowds as they arrive home at Victoria Station after their tour of Australia and New Zealand in June 1927.

22

ABOVE A charming etching of Queen Elizabeth, 1936.

RIGHT ABOVE A portrait of Her Majesty Queen Elizabeth in 1937 by T Martin Ronaldson.

OPPOSITE The two little princesses were a great asset to the Royal family and accompanied their mother on Royal visits whenever possible; here they are shown arriving at a Royal engagement with the Duchess of York.

OVERLEAF The two princesses pictured at the windows of the Welsh House, Windsor, in about 1936.

events of 1936-37. The Prince of Wales was living a secluded life at Fort Belvedere, his home near Virginia Water. He saw the Yorks less and less but remained a fond uncle to the little Princesses.

By 1935 all the King's sons were married except for Edward (or David as he was always known to his friends and family). Tired of waiting for his eldest son to make a suitable match, the King said to Prime Minister Stanley Baldwin in frustration: 'After I am dead, the boy will ruin himself in twelve months'. On 6 May 1935 the King and Queen, his darling 'May', drove in procession to St Paul's Cathedral for a service in celebration of his Silver Jubilee. The warmth and spontaneity of the crowds that greeted them delighted the King, who had not realized how very popular he was. Sadly, from this time onward the King's health, which had not been good for some years, began seriously to decline. By Christmas he was too ill to join in the family celebrations. In January he contracted a chill which immediately exacerbated his chest problems and weak heart. By January 20 he was clearly dying and the famous bulletin was announced on the wireless: 'The King's life is peacefully drawing to a close'. He died the same day and was buried at Windsor on January 28 1936.

It was Mrs Simpson who stood at the side of Edward VIII as he watched the pageantry of his proclamation as King from a window in St James's Palace. He was obsessively in love with her and was determined to make her his wife. In the tense, difficult months that preceded the Abdication, neither Elizabeth nor Bertie could believe that

the new King really meant to marry Wallis Simpson, who was twice married and in October 1936 became twice divorced. During a Mediterranean cruise with her, however, the King made little attempt to hide the true nature of their relationship which, thanks to a Gentleman's Agreement between the two major British press barons Lord Beaverbrook and Lord Rothermere, had been kept largely hidden from the public at home.

On October 20 the King told Baldwin that he intended to marry Wallis. Still everyone hoped that the crisis could be averted but on December 2, when the Yorks were returning from an official visit to Scotland, newspaper headlines screamed the news: 'KING TO MARRY WALLY'. As the Duchess of York said, the cat was out of the bag and nothing in the world would stuff it back. All attempts to change the King's mind failed. On December 10 King Edward VIII signed the instrument of Abdication. The severity of this blow to the Yorks cannot be overstated. The last few months had been an agonizing nightmare for them both. The Duke was, quite simply, appalled: 'This cannot be happening to me', he said. The doubts expressed about his ability to be King, and plans to perhaps substitute one of his brothers, only worsened his distress. Once she knew that the future of the monarchy would rest upon her husband's shoulders, Elizabeth bitterly resented their new role, more for his sake than for hers.

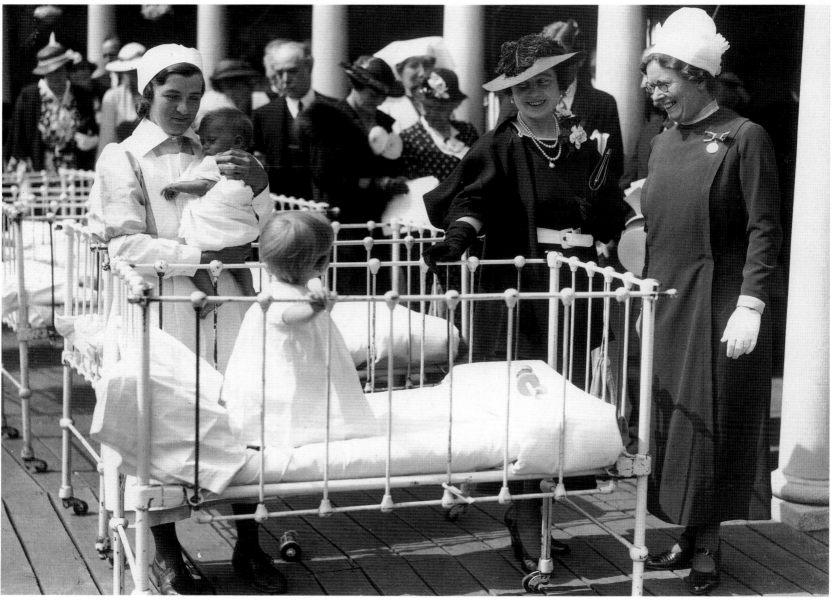

TOP AND ABOVE In the tense difficult months leading up to the Abdication, the Duke and Duchess did their best to carry on as normal and perform all their public duties as usual. The respite provided by private family life was needed more than ever.

OPPOSITE The Duchess poses with a favourite corgi in the grounds of 145 Piccadilly in the summer of 1936.

It had always been her philosophy to make the best of whatever life brought her and this massive, unexpected responsibility, which she termed an 'intolerable honour', proved to be no exception. In his Abdication Speech, Edward VIII told his people that he could not carry on as King without the 'help and support of the woman I love'. In his speech to the bewildered and anxious British public, his brother King George VI also included the woman he loved, as he vowed to serve his people as best he could: 'With my wife and helpmeet by my side I take up the heavy task that lies before me'. He felt overwhelmed and unprepared, telling Lord Mountbatten that 'I'm only a Naval Officer, it's the only thing I know how to do'. Nevertheless, he was King. He and Elizabeth now stood in what Lord Tennyson, in a poem written for Queen Victoria, called 'that fierce light that beats upon a throne'.

ROYAL QUEEN

In the aftermath of the Abdication Crisis, King George VI felt that it was up to him to restore the British people's faith in the monarchy. In a letter to Stanley Baldwin he wrote: 'I hope that time will be allowed to me to make amends for what has happened'. He had admired and worshipped his older brother all his life and now, suddenly, he was stepping into his shoes. He did, however, have the support of his loving wife and adoring daughters. The four of them moved into Buckingham Palace on February 15 1937. Life at 145 Piccadilly had been happy and tranquil, and the Queen was determined things would stay that way. She was a calm and very loving mother who brought her own unique brand of warmth and common sense into the previously rather austere method of bringing up Royal children. She began to change the way the Palace was run and abolished the antiquated custom of Royal children bowing to their parents. She inspired in others the confidence that had been hers since

OPPOSITE Six months into the War and the Queen finds time to play with one of her beloved corgis. During one of the many air raids at the time of the Blitz, a servant at Buckingham Palace observed the King rushing upstairs as the warning sounded, and then returning a few moments later with a reluctant corgi under his arm.

LEFT The Queen dressed in fashionable furs in 1944. Throughout the war she rejected the idea of wearing a uniform in favour of elegant but understated clothes which she believed would help boost public morale.

childhood. It soon became clear that she and the King were more than making up for the loss of Edward VIII. Harold Nicolson wrote in his diary after seeing them as King and Queen for the first time: 'What astonished me is how the King has changed. He is now like his brother. He was so gay and she so calm'.

The Coronation Day remained unchanged – May 12 1937. The man whose reign had been so brief was now known as His Royal Highness The Duke of Windsor, a title which had been the King's suggestion. Wallis, however, was refused the title of Royal Highness and this embittered her husband, who felt it was unfair. It was a difficult decision for the King and his advisors, and some historians have criticized it as being illegal. However, it must be remembered that no one knew how long the Windsors' marriage would last and once it has been bestowed the title of HRH cannot be revoked. King George VI showed himself to be steadfast and gracious in his dealings with his brother, who made a habit of ringing up from France (where he and Wallis had settled) to offer unwelcome advice on the skills of kingship. Elizabeth soon made sure he knew the phone calls had to stop.

Only five months passed between Elizabeth's accession and her Coronation. It was raining when, on May12 1937, the King and Queen endured a bumpy ride in the Gold State Coach from Buckingham Palace to Westminster Abbey. The King looked drawn and pale by the time they stepped out of the coach. Unsurprisingly one of the Prelates, sweltering in his long scarlet, woollen cloak, fainted and had to be hurriedly helped away so that the procession could continue. Both the King and Queen felt that the Coronation changed them forever; they believed it gave them new understanding and optimism. Observers noticed their trancelike expressions as the crowns were placed on their heads. When the ceremony was over they felt exhausted, but very much relieved that this tumultuous day had passed. The King gave Elizabeth a very special gift – a glittering Badge and Star of diamonds, emeralds, and sapphires, investing her as the only Lady of the Garter that there has ever been. Later in the evening the King made a radio broadcast to his people to thank them for their support. He described May 12 as 'this day of inspiration which the Queen and I will always keep in ours hearts'.

Both their lives changed radically when they became King and Queen; their privacy and freedom were more restricted, but the effect of the Abdication on their children was much more difficult to bear. They did their best to ensure they saw as much of them as before but inevitably time was scarcer now and only weekends at Royal Lodge remained the same. 'Nothing in the Abdication cut so deep as the changed future for their children – it was hardest of all for their sake,' wrote Sir David Bowes-Lyon, the

RIGHT The Queen, with Princess Elizabeth and Princess Margaret, in relaxed mood on the garden steps at Windsor Castle in July 1941. It is hard to believe that this is the woman Hitler termed 'the most dangerous' in Europe.

ABOVE A watercolour portrait of Queen Elizabeth at Windsor Castle, July 8 1941.

TOP The Queen and Queen Mary enter the Mall at the Trooping of the Colour, June 1937.

RIGHT The King and Queen leaving the Tate Gallery in London after opening the new sculpture extension. The Queen Mother has always been a great patron of the arts; her private collection includes paintings by Monet, Sickert, Sisley, Nash, Lowry and Duncan Grant.

Queen's brother. The King and Queen also spent less time together as the interminable Royal Boxes and mass of routine paper work occupied the King for many hours in the day and the Queen spent a good deal of her time at her desk. If they had to be apart, then the King would phone her, sometimes talking for over an hour. They worked very much in partnership; Queen Elizabeth knew about all State Business that concerned the King and was much more aware of affairs of state than either Queen Alexandra or Queen Mary. When it came to planning Royal tours, the King and Queen would sit down with their Private Secretaries and plan them together.

As his workload increased, so the King needed Elizabeth more and more. What has been noted much less frequently is how much she depended on him. Theirs was a mutually dependent, loving and very equal partnership. Lady Rose Granville, the Queen's sister, made the following comment on their marriage: 'They were so particularly together. The King was a rock to her, indeed to all of us. In fundamental things she leant on him. I have always felt how much the Queen was sustained by the King'.

Queen Elizabeth made the housing problem one of her special interests. She made a series of visits to the poor parts of London to see the slum conditions and the measures being taken to relieve them. She was keen to see everything, especially the kitchens where she would chat to the housewives and sometimes stay for a cup of tea. She and the King became experts on many of the social problems of the 1930s. In 1938 they visited Glasgow to open the Empire Exhibition and insisted on visiting the housing schemes in Renfrewshire and Lanarkshire. They took care to involve themselves in the various Ministry of Employment training schemes for the unemployed. The King had always been progressive politically and relished the opportunity to put into practice what had previously been only theories.

On June 28 1938 the Queen's mother, Lady Strathmore, died after a long illness. Queen Elizabeth did not have the chance to grieve privately for very long as a tour of France had been arranged; departure was delayed until July 19. The Queen's wardrobe had already been designed by her new Court dressmaker, Norman Hartnell. Happily,

34

ABOVE An early colour photograph of the Royal Family taken at Buckingham Palace in May 1942. The Queen always ensured that their time together was as relaxed and private as possible.

RIGHT A study of the King and Queen taken in 1947 at Buckingham Palace. Here the King looks as relaxed as he ever did in public photos but the war had left him feeling 'burnt out' and vulnerable to ill health.

an all-black wardrobe was avoided when Hartnell remembered that white was also a traditional colour of mourning, and the Queen's new dresses were all hurriedly re-made. As the Duchess of York, the Queen's wardrobe had been pretty and charming without being ultra chic. Now the King wanted her to have her own unique look. He showed Hartnell the pictures of Empress Eugénie of France, wife of Napoleon III, in her billowing crinoline dresses as painted by Franz Winterhalter, a very popular painter of the aristocracy in the mid-nineteenth century. He wanted Hartnell to cap-ture the paintings' 'picturesque grace'.

The tour of France was another great success for the Royal couple. The Queen looked superb in her romantic, frothy, waisted dresses. The French pronounced them-selves stunned and captivated – one newspaper headline read: 'We have taken the Queen to our hearts. She rules over two nations'. Mme Lebrun, wife of the French President, wrote to the Queen after her visit: 'I wish to assure Your Majesty that she has won the hearts of the whole of Paris'. The dark clouds of war were present through-out the visit. At Versailles the King reviewed 50,000 of France's best troops. Rum-blings of war had haunted the King and Queen since their Coronation. The British people were slow to take an interest in the affairs of the rest of Europe and it seemed that Neville Chamberlain's policy of appeasement was working well. But in March

ABOVE The Royal ladies
watching the presenting of
the new Colors to the
Grenadier Guards at
Buckingham Palace in May
1938.

RIGHT The Queen in
Paris wearing one of the
fabulous Winterhalter
dresses designed for her by
Hartnell, during the tour of
France in July 1938.

1938 Hitler marched into Austria and in September he invaded Czechoslovakia, pre-
cipitating Chamberlain's infamous dash to meet the Nazi dictator. He returned with
the empty promise of 'Peace in our Time'. The King liked and trusted Chamberlain,
but even as they stood together on the balcony of Buckingham Palace, to the acclaim
of the cheering crowds below them, it was obvious to many people that war could not
be avoided.

The King and Queen's next major task was the very important tour of Canada and
the USA, important because, in the event of war, Britain would be much in need of
the support of these two countries. It was the first visit of a reigning British Monarch
and his consort to Canada. The two little Princesses had been invited, but it was
decided that the tour would be too strenuous for them so they stayed behind. The King
and Queen left Southampton on May 5 1939 on board the Empress of Australia. King
Edward VIII had been enormously popular in Canada, even buying a ranch in Alberta
when he was Prince of Wales. The Duke of York had been far less well known. Fears of
a half-hearted reaction proved unfounded, however, as they were well received
wherever they went. As always, the schedule was hectic and very hard work; the King
and Queen covered 4281 miles on Canada's national railways. The Queen loved

Canada, a country she visited many times as Queen Mother. She undertook several engagements herself, presenting colours to the Toronto Scottish Regiment on the campus of Toronto University and laying the foundation stone of the new Supreme Court building in Ottawa, where she made a very successful speech partly in French.

The visit to the United States included the first made by a King of England to Washington where, as in all other American cities, many people were determined to remain neutral should hostilities break out in Europe. President Roosevelt, however, realized how vital the partnership between his country and Britain was, and he invited the King and Queen to his private home in an attempt to bring the two countries closer together. The visit took place in soaring temperatures which reached 100°F at times, and the humidity made it seem even hotter. The enthusiasm of the crowds matched the warmth of the weather. After a visit to Congress, one Senator, a fervent isolationist, chatted happily to the Queen and then congratulated the King on being a 'very good Queen picker'. After the visit to the World Fair in New York, the Royal party drove out to the Roosevelts' private country home at Hyde Park. The King and the President took to each other straight away. Despite the late hour of 8 pm the President's mother insisted on serving tea. 'My mother does not approve of cocktails', the

OVERLEAF King George VI and Queen Elizabeth photographed in Buckingham Palace during World War II. The Queen was determined that she and her family should remain in Britain throughout the war. She even learnt to use a gun, declaring 'I shall not go down like the others'.

LEFT By August 1941
Windsor Great Park had
been ploughed up to grow
much needed food for the
war effort. Here and below
the Royal Family inspect
the crop at harvest time.

President explained. 'Neither does mine,' the King smiled back as they comforted themselves later with a stiff drink.

Amid all the fun and pleasantries the two men found time to discuss the very real possibility of war, and how America could help Britain if (or by this stage when) it broke out. Their important mission accomplished, the King and Queen returned to Canada on the next day to finish the tour there. They returned home on June 22, Princess Elizabeth and Princess Margaret joining them on board ship as the *Empress of Britain* approached Southampton. The success of the tour, with its informal moments and pictures of the King and Queen enjoying hotdogs and barbecues and drinking beer, drew the Royal couple closer to the British people and helped to demystify the Monarchy. The crowds were ecstatic as the Royal boat train drew into Waterloo. The streets were lined with people and MPs stood in Parliament Square to watch the King and Queen drive back to Buckingham Palace. Elizabeth and Bertie were modestly pleased with their triumph – the King believed 'this has made us'.

The inevitable finally occured on September 3 1939, the day World War Two was declared. The King and Queen made a resolute and much praised decision to stay in Britain and resist the suggestions that they and their daughters move to Canada or elsewhere for the duration of the war. The Queen was horrified at the idea of leaving – 'I should die if I had to leave,' she declared firmly. The Princesses did move to Windsor Castle where they were guarded by twelve young officers from the Brigade of Guards. The King and Queen would stay at Windsor at night whenever possible, but would always depart for London at 8.00 sharp in the morning. They travelled 50,000 miles around Britain during the war, visiting hospitals, military barracks, bomb-damaged towns and cities, Home Guard Stations – in fact everywhere in need of the Sovereign's support. On September 7 1940 London was bombed for the first time; the Battle of Britain had begun in earnest. The King and Queen visited as many of London's bomb sites as they could. On September 12 Buckingham Palace was bombed and the King

42

ABOVE   Queen Elizabeth
and King George VI in
carefully posed informality,
having tea at Buckingham
Palace.

RIGHT   The King and
Queen inspect a Civil
Defence Parade during
World War II.

OPPOSITE   The King and
Queen at Buckingham
Palace, 1947. The King is
standing by one of the red
boxes whose state papers
would occupy him for so
many hours each day.

and Queen had a very fortunate escape. The King wrote in his diary: 'It was a ghastly experience and I don't want it to be repeated' (in fact the Palace was bombed another eight times).

When Eleanor Roosevelt visited Buckingham Palace in October 1942, she was able to observe that the Royal Family were not enjoying privileges that their subjects were forced to forego. The King had drawn a plimsoll line of five inches around the bath, and Mrs Roosevelt found everywhere in the Palace, including the Queen's bedroom in which she was sleeping, cold and drafty as the building had lost so many of its windows through bomb damage. She was surprised to be served regulation war rations such as dried egg and Woolten pie – albeit on gold and silver platters.

The King felt continually frustrated at missing the war action but did at least manage to visit his troops in north Africa, against the wishes of his advisors. He was very disappointed at not being allowed to accompany the D-Day assault force when it sailed for the Normandy beaches on June 6 1944. But he did join the troops in France ten days later for a morale-boosting tour of the soldiers. When the war finally ended in 1945 the King and his country were both worn out. In 1940 the King had written: 'I feel quite exhausted after seeing so much sadness, sorrow, heroism and magnificent spirit', and now his intense sense of duty and feelings for his people had taken their toll. On VE Day, the King and Queen, the two Princesses and Prime Minister Winston Churchill (whom the King had come to admire very much), stood on the balcony of Buckingham Palace to wave to the joyous crowds celebrating the end of the war. There were eight 'curtain calls' altogether.

By the end of the war Princess Elizabeth was nineteen and very much in love with a young naval cadet, Prince Philip of Greece. She was set on marrying him but her parents felt she was too young and inexperienced for such a big step. So a bargain was struck – Princess Elizabeth would accompany the rest of the Royal family on a trip to South Africa in early 1947; when they returned, she would be free to marry. They left for South Africa on February 1 1947 for what proved to be a very strenuous tour in

RIGHT *It was not all gloom during the war. Here the King and Queen and Duchesses of Kent and Gloucester attend a performance of Black Velvet in January 1939.*

BELOW *This delightful study of the Queen posing in the country in July 1941 shows her determination still to wear pretty, pastel shades despite the austerity of the time.*

OPPOSITE *The Queen with Princess Margaret and Princess Elizabeth at Windsor Castle in May 1944. Princess Elizabeth had celebrated her eighteenth birthday a month before and had insisted on joining the ATS to do 'what other girls of my age do'.*

OVERLEAF *The Queen at the Derby races, Epsom 1947: although already a keen racegoer she did not become an owner until the following year.*

44

which the Royal family travelled thousands of miles in the unfortunately named White Train. Philip became a British subject on February 28 1947, renouncing his rights of succession to the Greek and Danish thrones and adopting the surname of Mountbatten, and the engagement was announced two months after his fiancée's return, on July 10 1947. The wedding was a chance for people to enjoy the much missed Royal pageantry. Although very happy that his daughter had found love, the King was sad to see his beloved 'Lillibet' leave home.

Five months later, the King and Queen celebrated their silver wedding anniversary. This happy event, and the news that Princess Elizabeth was expecting a baby, co-incided with the worrying diagnosis that the severe pains and cramps that the King had been suffering in his legs was caused by arteriosclerosis. It was a difficult time for the Queen, who decided that the news should be kept from Princess Elizabeth until she had had her baby at Buckingham Palace (where she and Prince Philip had lived since they were married). While the King lay ill in bed, Prince Charles was born on November 14 1948. In spring 1949 his doctors announced that the King needed an

48

THE QUEEN

Established 1861

Volume 185. No. 4838

Wednesday, September 13th, 1939

Photo: MARCUS ADAMS

THEY ARE MOTHER AND FATHER, TOO

King George and Queen Elizabeth, while they are playing a big part in the life of this strange new London, must often find their thoughts turning, just as those of other parents are doing, to the two little daughters they have had to leave behind in the greater safety of the country

OPPOSITE ABOVE The Queen with nurses and patients outside her family home of St Paul's Walden Bury in Hertfordshire (it was turned into a military hospital during World War II).

OPPOSITE BELOW The Queen chatting to WAAF girls on a surprise visit to a balloon site in March 1943.

LEFT One of the many official photographs of the Royal family used to inspire the war effort.

BELOW The Queen in one of her chic wartime outfits, at Royal Lodge April 1940.

49

operation to free the circulation in his right leg. With plenty of rest he recuperated well, but in September 1951 he had to undergo tests on his lungs. 'Now they think there's something wrong with me blowers', he moaned. The results were a great shock; the King had lung cancer and it was projected that he would only live another eighteen months. The King was never told the true nature of his illness. He underwent a lung resection operation on September 23 and by Christmas was strong enough to go shooting at Balmoral, wearing electrically heated gloves and boots. On January 30 1952, the King and Queen and Princess Margaret travelled to the airport to see off Princess Elizabeth and her husband, who were leaving for Kenya en route for a Commonwealth tour of Australia. The King presented a sorrowful picture as he stood on the tarmac, hands dug deep in his pockets, watching his daughter's plane disappear to nothing in the sky.

February 5 1952 was the Keepers' Day Shoot at Sandringham, a favourite date in the King's calender. The Queen and Princess Margaret left to visit local artist Edward Seago at his riverside home at Ludlam. On their return the Queen hurried upstairs to see the King, who was resting in bed. She showed him the paintings Seago had given her as gifts, and after dinner the King retired back to bed, saying 'I'll see you in the morning'. The next morning his valet found him dead in bed at 7.15 am.

He had died in the night from a coronary thrombosis. The Queen insisted a vigil was kept outside his bedroom door, and went downstairs to break the news to Princess Margaret. Far away at Treetops in Kenya, it fell to Prince Philip to take Princess Elizabeth for a walk along the river and tell her she was now Queen.

50

ABOVE Queen Elizabeth
photographed at
Buckingham Palace in
1947.

LEFT A Silver Wedding
photograph of the King and
Queen, taken at
Buckingham Palace in
1947.

RIGHT The Royal Family
photographed together in
1947.

52

LEFT   The King and Queen in the Order of the Garter procession, April 1948. The occasion saw the installation of Princess Elizabeth and Prince Philip into the Order.

ABOVE   The Queen and Princess Margaret see Let's Make an Opera in December 1949.

RIGHT   The Royal Family on the way to Waterloo Station for their departure to South Africa in January 1947.

LEFT Conversation
Piece by Sir James Gunn,
painted at Royal Lodge,
Windsor, in 1950.

ABOVE The Queen and
Princess Margaret make an
impromptu visit to
Highland Home Industries,
Edinburgh, in July 1947.

RIGHT Royal Silver
Wedding Commemorative
stamp.

OVERLEAF King George
VI and Queen Elizabeth at
the opening of the Festival
of Britain, May 19 1951.

£1 1923-1948

58

FAR LEFT The Queen's
Working Party at
Buckingham Palace made
surgical dressings and
clothes for the Red Cross
during World War II.

LEFT The Queen and
Queen Mary at the Festival
of Britain, May 1951.

FAR LEFT The Queen
chats to children during one
of her visits to bomb
damage sites in London,
September 1940.

LEFT The Queen meets
children in a deep air raid
shelter in London in
November 1940.

60

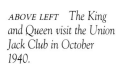

TOP The King and Queen at the Royal Command Performance in November 1949. The Queen is chatting to one of the programme sellers after the show.

ABOVE LEFT The King and Queen visit the Union Jack Club in October 1940.

ABOVE RIGHT Arriving for the race meeting on Derby Day 1950.

RIGHT The Queen with her studious daughters in the garden of Windsor Castle during World War II.

THE GLORIOUS
AFTERMATH

The funeral of King George VI was on February 15 1952, a miserable, wet, gray day. A naval party drew the King's coffin in a green gun carriage from the door of Westminster Hall, where it had lain in state. The new Queen had sent her father a floral bouquet from Kenya with the message: 'To my darling Papa, from your sorrowing Lillibet'. Her mother's floral tribute of white flowers lay on top of the coffin, with the words: 'To my dear husband, a great and noble King'. The coffin was taken to Paddington Station where Queen Elizabeth II, Princess Margaret, and the widowed Queen Elizabeth stood huddled together on the platform in their black mourning veils, while the bands of the Coldstream and Scots Guards played Chopin's *Funeral March*. The King's final journey was to St George's Chapel at Windsor Castle.

In his last Christmas radio broadcast, the King had spoken of the unchanging nature of the family: 'At Christmas we feel that the old simple things matter most,' he

ABOVE The Queen Mother on a Royal visit to Scotland in May 1969.

RIGHT The Queen Mother and Prince Charles taking part in the annual Knights of the Garter procession and service at Windsor Castle.

OPPOSITE The Queen Mother outside Clarence House on her 88th birthday. The annual presentation of flowers and cards from children has become a firmly established tradition.

64

ABOVE The Queen Mother and Princess Margaret leave for Southern Rhodesia in June 1953. It was hoped that the trip would distract the Princess from her troubled romance with Peter Townsend.

OPPOSITE King George VI's funeral coffin arrives at St George's Chapel Windsor, February 15 1952.

said, 'they do not change, however much the world outside may seem to do so'. With his death Elizabeth's life changed forever. She was suddenly no longer Queen but the mother of the Queen; a dramatic change in roles. She chose to be known as Queen Elizabeth the Queen Mother, rejecting the antiquated term of 'Dowager Queen'. She was devastated by her husband's death. He had been her closest companion for very nearly 30 years and now she was a widow at the age of 51. Still numb from her loss, she wrote to the painter Edward Seago: 'One still can't quite believe it has all happened. One feels rather dazed'. The public were absorbed in their sympathies for the vulnerable young Queen. Few people realized how isolated and alone the Queen Mother felt. One friend who did was Edith Sitwell, who sent her an anthology of poetry which included a poem by the seventeenth century clergyman and poet George Herbert. In her thankyou letter, Elizabeth reflected on the poet's phrase 'How small and selfish is sorrow', but, as she added: 'It bangs one about until one is senseless'.

In her message to the nation the Queen Mother asked the public to support her daughter as 'in the great and lonely station to which she has been called, she will need your protection and your love'. For herself, she withdrew from the public gaze for many months following the King's death. In the autumn of 1953 Winston Churchill, a trusted confidant, paid her a surprise visit at Birkhall, her Highland home, while he was at Balmoral. She has never revealed what he said to her but her return to the public arena dates from that time. She and Princess Margaret swapped homes with the Queen and Prince Philip they moved into Buckingham Palace and, a year later, the Queen Mother and her younger daughter moved down the Mall into Clarence House, which has remained her London residence ever since.

It was in the early years of her widowhood that the Queen Mother discovered the Castle of Mey. The story goes that while she was visiting her friends Commander Clare and Lady Doris Vyner at Caithness in Scotland, she spotted the little castle when she was out for a drive. When she discovered that it was due to be demolished, as no buyers were interested, she decided to buy it herself. This she did, restoring its ancient name of the Castle of Mey (instead of Barrogil). Its renovation and restoration

ABOVE LEFT Norman Hartnell's design for the dress worn by the Queen Mother at her daughter's Coronation in 1952.

ABOVE RIGHT The Queen Mother pictured at a Royal garden party at Buckingham Palace in 1955.

OPPOSITE The Queen Mother with Princess Anne and Prince Charles in 1951. She has been a source of constant support and advice to her grandchildren through the years.

(a massive undertaking) became a labour of love which in return restored her interest in life and living. She still spends much of August in this very private home, which she loves; buying it was a return to her Scottish roots. The remoteness and wildness of Caithness refreshes her after her busy, public life in the centre of London.

On March 1953 Queen Mary, widow of George V, died surrounded by all her family (including the Duke of Windsor but not the Duchess). The loss greatly saddened the Queen Mother, as her mother-in-law had always been loyal and helpful to her. The Coronation of Queen Elizabeth II followed ten weeks later on June 2 1953. It was the Queen Mother's task to entertain four-year old Prince Charles during the ceremony; she managed to keep him quiet by rummaging in her handbag and answering his questions in low whispers. She felt very moved to witness her daughter experience the same sense of religious dedication and mystery that she and her husband had undergone 16 years earlier.

Princess Margaret was a source of companionship, delightful wit but also real worry for the Queen Mother during the 1950s. She had fallen in love with Group Captain Peter Townsend, her late father's equerry, and a divorced man 16 years her senior. The Royal Marriages Act of 1772 ensured that Princess Margaret could not marry without the Sovereign's permission until she was 25. Winston Churchill, who was Prime Minister again and a great romantic, had to put his own feelings aside when he informed the Queen Mother that he felt it very unlikely Parliament would agree to the marriage. Finally it was agreed that Townsend should go to Brussels for two years to take up the position of British Air Attaché. On his return, Margaret would be free to marry him without her sister having to give her permission. Unfortunately, when he did return he and Margaret learnt from Anthony Eden, the new Prime Minister, that a majority in Parliament was still against the match, so the couple gave up the fight, knowing how impossible their situation was. Princess Margaret made a public announcement renouncing her intention to marry Townsend; the statement had been drafted for her the evening before by the man she was being forced to reject.

In his book *Time and Chance*, Peter Townsend wrote about the Queen Mother's attitude toward him during the whole affair: 'She was never anything but considerate in her attitude to me. She never once hurt either of us throughout the whole difficult time'. However, her private distress can be measured by the report that she burst into tears when telling her private household that her daughter wanted to marry

Townsend. In the late 1950s, Peter Townsend married a Belgian girl, and on May 6 1960 Princess Margaret married Anthony Armstrong Jones (or Lord Snowdon, as he was especially created). They had two children, David, Viscount Linley, and Lady Sarah Armstrong Jones. They were divorced in 1976.

In 1953 the Queen Mother began her extensive world travels. She was the first Royal to travel around the world. In June 1953 she and Princess Margaret, who was sitting out the difficult waiting period for Peter Townsend, visited Rhodesia as part of the celebrations for the centenary of the birth of Cecil Rhodes. Princess Margaret caught a bad dose of flu and had to come home but the Queen Mother sailed through, undertaking 54 engagements and travelling 15,000 miles. In 1954 she embarked on a long tour of Canada and the US. She had been invited to New York to accept a cheque on behalf of the George VI Memorial Fund, a charitable foundation set up by Lew Douglas, pre-war Ambassador to London, which had the support of President Eisenhower. Its aims were to collect money to help train young men and women from the Commonwealth in American colleges and universities.

The Queen Mother set sail on October 21 on board the liner *Queen Elizabeth*, which she had launched before the war. Few people expected the tour to be a triumph, as Queen Elizabeth the Queen Mother was a middle-aged widow and few Americans were interested in any Royal other than her daughter the Queen. The visit began modestly but the crowds grew bigger and bigger as news of the charming visitor spread. She received the George VI Memorial Fund cheque at a televized banquet at the Waldorf Astoria Hotel in New York. She was very keen to visit some of New York's famous shops, and when she did so was amazed at the number of people who turned out hoping

BELOW The Queen Mother, Princess Margaret, Lord Snowdon and the Princess Royal on Derby Day, June 1952.

RIGHT The Castle of Mey, bought by the Queen Mother in 1952 as a very special private retreat.

FAR RIGHT ABOVE The Queen Mother attending gundog trials in Scotland in 1973.

FAR RIGHT BELOW An enthusiastic Queen Mother watching the racing with the Queen on Derby Day 1985.

68

70

to get a glimpse of her. The tour was a major step forward for the Queen Mother; she very much enjoyed the public acclaim it brought her and it renewed her enthusiasm for her continuing role in public life.

In 1955 the Queen Mother took another major step back into the public spotlight when she became Chancellor of London University. It was a major undertaking and one she always found very enjoyable. She showed a genuine interest and concern in the affairs of the students, always lending her invaluable support to any fund-raising activities, from jumble sales to campaigns for new buildings. She read reports, attended student dances, visited union centres and halls of residence, always with enthusiasm. All the previous chancellors had retired at 75 and when the Queen Mother announced that she had decided to carry on, at the Foundation Day Dinner in 1975, everyone present was delighted. When she did retire in 1980, her granddaughter Princess Anne took over the position.

Any member of the public asked to name a sport connected with the Queen Mother would undoutedly choose racing. Her interest in the sport began in 1949 when she and Princess Elizabeth bought a nine-year-old steeple chaser called Monaveen. This Irish-bred horse was the first of several very good horses that the Queen Mother owned over the next few decades. Sadly, Monaveen fell and broke a leg at Hurst Park in 1950 and had to be destroyed. Princess Elizabeth was so upset she abandoned steeplechasing for the flat but her mother continued and bought Manicou in the same year. She raced him and all her horses in the Strathmore colors; the jockey wore pale blue jacket with buff stripes, pale blue sleeves and black cap with gold tassel. When Manicou won at Kempton Park in November of that year, it was the first time a Queen had won the race since Queen Anne in 1714. The Queen Mother's favourite horse was The Rip (sired by Manicou) who, with Laffy and Double Star, won her first racing hattrick. Her success continued, with her heyday being the 1960s when she had up to 15 horses in training. What began as a distraction to help her cope with the King's illness be-

ABOVE The Queen Mother hugs Prince Charles as she arrives home at Waterloo station in November 1951 from her tour of the USA.

RIGHT The Queen Mother loves racing and never objects to the cold weather. Here she is wrapped up against the cold wind at Sandown in December 1963.

OVERLEAF The Queen Mother in Sydney during her Royal tour of Australia in 1958.

RIGHT   The Queen and the Queen Mother standing on the steps of St George's Chapel, Windsor, after the funeral service for Princess Alice (last of Queen Victoria's 37 grandchildren) in January 1981.

ABOVE   The Queen Mother and her daughter very much enjoy the country life.

ABOVE RIGHT   The Queen Mother at the Silver Jubilee Service in Westminster Abbey on October 30 1973.

came a lifelong devotion. The Queen Mother is able to feel relaxed on the racecourse, where the thrill of the race is a great release from the staged routine of Royal life.

The Queen Mother has an infectious love of life. She is as capable of finding pleasure in the simple pursuits of gardening, parlour games and her favourite card games as she is in her travels abroad. The countries she has visited are too numerous to list but they include Italy, Tunisia, Germany, Iran, Uganda, Mauritius, the islands of the Carribean, Norway, and Hawaii. She remains as active as ever and lives life at a pace which would punish many people half her age. The Queen Mother often shows us the human face of Royalty and excels at putting people at their ease. When a guest was once embarrassingly late for dinner at Clarence House, she merely smiled and said: 'It was lovely, for once I could catch the whole of *Dad's Army*'.

She has worked long and hard to ensure that the Royal Family retain their valued place in the nation's affections. It is very hard to imagine the Monarchy without her steadfast and tranquil presence. She commands respect and admiration in all her dealings. Above all, she has endured with grace and dignity. One of the few criticisms levelled at her is her attitude to the Duchess of Windsor, but no one can doubt that it was out of concern for her husband, who was trying to repair the rift that the abdication had opened up, that she was determined the Windsors should not return to Britain; she felt their presence would only undermine the King's position. When the Duke died from throat cancer in 1972 she spoke gently and kindly to the Duchess at his funeral. In 1976 she did her best to cease hostilities when she sent the Duchess two dozen red roses and a message which read 'In friendship, Elizabeth'. Wallis died from a heart attack in 1986 after many years of incapacitating illness. As she had so fervently wished, she was buried beside her husband at Windsor Castle.

No one has ever written a more fitting or personal tribute to the Queen Mother than

LEFT The Queen Mother enjoys a gondola ride during her trip to Venice to aid the Venice in Peril Fund in 1984.

TOP The Queen Mother pictured during her tour of Australia in 1958.

ABOVE The Australian four was one of the Queen Mother's first solo successes.

Prince Charles, who chose the following words to express his feelings for his grandmother: 'For me she has always been one of those extraordinary, rare people whose touch can turn everything to gold . . . She belongs to that priceless brand of people whose greatest gift is to enhance life for others, through her own effervescent enthusiasm for life'. For her eightieth birthday, the Poet Laureate, Sir John Betjeman wrote her a commemerative poem which included the lines:

> Waves of goodwill
> Go racing to meet you . . .

These words came true once again in August 1990 when the nation celebrated her ninetieth birthday. The far more ancient words chosen to describe the enduring strength of the Royal Family, gathered in St Paul's Cathedral for a service in celebration of the Queen and Prince Philip's silver wedding in 1972, perfectly symbolize what the Queen Mother has meant over the years to the Monarchy. The Canon in Residence read the Second Lesson:

> And the rain descended and the floods came,
> And the winds blew, and beat upon that house,
> And it fell not; for it was built upon a rock.

There can be no doubt that the Queen Mother is the rock upon which the Royal Family is built. It is her steel-like strength and sense of moral purpose that has helped it to withstand so much change and indeed to flourish in this modern age.

ABOVE The Queen Mother receives birthday gifts from children outside Clarence House; the Queen and Princess Margaret help take the flowers as other members of the Royal Family look on.

RIGHT ABOVE The Queen Mother chats to a soldier at the Royal Tournament in July 1983.

RIGHT BELOW The Queen Mother smiles at an unexpected show of gallantry from a porter on a visit to Smithfield meat market in April 1982.

OPPOSITE The Queen Mother dressed in a favourite shade of blue.

THIS PAGE The Queen Mother continues to be active in entertaining visiting heads of state and making state visits.

ABOVE The Queen Mother, the Queen and Prince Philip with King Hassan of Morocco at a banquet in the King's honour in August 1987.

LEFT The Queen Mother with François Mitterand during her visit to Paris, 1982.

THIS PAGE AND OVERLEAF Official duties take many forms – only a few are shown here.

OPPOSITE ABOVE The Queen Mother presents shamrock to the Irish Guards in March 1987.

OPPOSITE BELOW 90th birthday tribute celebrations in 1990.

ABOVE The Queen Mother rides in a carriage with her grandson William at the Trooping of the Colour in June 1987.

BELOW Attending the Festival of Remembrance at the Albert Hall in November 1984.

OVERLEAF The Queen Mother is Warden of the Cinque Ports, five ports on the south coast of England which have had special duties and privileges since Anglo-Saxon times. She is here inspecting the troops at Dover in July 1979.

86

THIS PAGE AND OVERLEAF The Queen Mother's birthday is always the occasion for celebration, both formal and informal.

TOP The Queen Mother cuts a cake baked for her 80th birthday by the Army Catering Corps.

ABOVE The Queen Mother and the Queen enjoying the celebrations for her 80th birthday in 1980 outside Clarence House.

RIGHT The Queen Mother and Prince Charles ride to the Thanksgiving Service for her 80th birthday in July 1980. She has always been especially close to her eldest grandson.

88

ABOVE The Queen Mother celebrating her 80th birthday.

FAR LEFT The front cover of the brochure for the 90th birthday Military and Associated Civilian Organisations procession in June 1990.

LEFT AND RIGHT The Queen Mother on her 90th birthday.

90

LEFT ABOVE Prince
Charles and Princess Anne
with the Queen Mother
holding a baby Prince
Andrew on the day of his
christening in 1960.

LEFT BELOW Another
family group showing the
Queen Mother with Prince
Edward and Princess
Margaret's children Lady
Sarah Armstrong Jones and
David, Viscount Linley.

TOP The Royal Family
gathered together for the
christening of Princess
Anne's first child, Peter
Phillips.

ABOVE LEFT The Queen
and the Queen Mother
attending morning service
at Sandringham.

ABOVE RIGHT The Royal
Family attending morning
service on Christmas Day
at St George's Chapel,
Windsor in 1967.

92

ABOVE A formal group photograph of the Royal Family at Princess Anne's wedding to Captain Mark Phillips in 1973.

RIGHT Prince Edward and the Queen Mother ride to St Paul's Cathedral for the wedding of Princess Charles and Lady Diana Spencer in July 1981.

OPPOSITE ABOVE Inside St Paul's after the wedding ceremony.

OPPOSITE BELOW Another Royal Wedding; the Duchess of York teases the crowd as the Royal Family gather on the balcony after her marriage to Prince Andrew in the summer of 1986.

94

LEFT The Queen Mother is a very keen theatre goer. Here she attends the Royal Opera House, Covent Garden for a gala performance of Sleeping Beauty, in 1968.

BELOW She especially enjoys musicals and ballet and here she meets the cast of High Society at a gala performance in February 1987.

LEFT Meeting the Jackson Five at the Royal Variety Performance in 1972.

RIGHT At the Royal Opera House in 1963.

ABOVE   More bright lights and famous personalities; the Queen Mother talks to Luciano Pavarotti at the Royal Albert Hall.

LEFT   Shaking hands with the Supremes at the Royal Variety Performance in 1968.

RIGHT   With Princess Anne and Princess Margaret at the Royal Variety Performance in 1972.

98

ABOVE   The Queen
Mother with her two
youngest grandchildren
Prince Andrew and Prince
Edward in St Paul's
Cathedral on the occasion
of the Queen's Silver
Jubilee in 1977.

RIGHT   With all six
grandchildren – clockwise
from left, Princess Anne,
Prince Edward, Prince
Charles, Prince Andrew,
Viscount Linley and Lady
Sarah Armstrong-Jones –
in 1980.

OPPOSITE ABOVE A host of public engagements for the working grandmother; opening the Syon House garden centre in June 1968.

OPPOSITE BELOW Elegant in evening dress.

LEFT ABOVE Playing pool at a Jersey youth club in 1986.

LEFT BELOW Visiting Sainsbury's on the Cromwell Road, London, in 1985.

TOP At the Royal Smithfield Show in 1987.

ABOVE Wearing a favourite style of hat, Welwyn Garden City 1970.

102

ABOVE Formal occasions:
the Queen Mother and
Prince Charles at the
Garter Service, St George's
Chapel Windsor.

LEFT Receiving an
honorary Doctor of Music
degree from the Royal
College of Music in 1973.

RIGHT Resplendent in
green velvet for a visit to
Lloyds of London in 1987.

104

TOP Opening the new art department at Chigwell school in January 1981.

ABOVE With Harold Macmillan and James Callaghan at the unveiling of the statue of Viscount Montgomery in 1980.

RIGHT With Princess Anne, Princess Margaret and Lord Snowdon at the Investiture of Prince Charles as Prince of Wales.

LEFT Sporting life: the Queen Mother with the Princess of Wales at Ascot in 1987.

ABOVE With the Queen, the Prince and Princess of Wales, and the Duchess of York at the Braemar Games in 1987.

RIGHT Suitably clad at the Badminton Horse Trials.

108

LEFT The Queen Mother at the Festival of Remembrance in Westminster Abbey, 1983.

BELOW With Prince and Princess Michael of Kent at Badminton in 1982.

RIGHT A rare moment of solitude for the Queen Mother, walking one of her dogs.

OVERLEAF The Queen Mother, a formal and an informal view.

ACKNOWLEDGMENTS

The publisher would like to thank Mike Rose, who designed this book and Jessica Orebi Gann, the project editor. We would also like to thank the following individuals and institutions for supplying illustrative material.

Anwar Hussein, pages 1, 2, 63, 69 (top right), 76, 82 (bottom), 88 (bottom left and right), 89, 91 (top), 93 (bottom), 101 (top left), 109, 110

Hulton-Deutsch Collection, pages 4/5, 6, 8, 9 (both), 11 (top), 12 (bottom), 13 (bottom), 15 (left), 16, 17 (both), 18 (both), 19, 20, 21 (both), 22 (both), 23, 24/5, 26 (both), 27, 28, 29, 30/31, 32 (both), 33, 34, 35, 36, 37, 38/39, 40, 41, 42 (both), 43, 44 (both), 45, 46/47, 48 (both), 49 (bottom), 50 (both), 51, 52, 53 (both), 55 (both), 56/57, 58 (both), 59 (both), 60 (all), 61, 62 (both), 64, 65, 66 (both), 67, 68, 69 (top right and bottom), 70, 71, 72/73, 74, 75 (both), 77 (both), 78, 79 (both), 80, 81 (both), 82 (top), 83 (both), 84/85, 86 (both), 87, 88 (top), 90 (both), 91 (bottom left and right), 92 (both), 93 (top), 94 (all), 95, 96 (both), 97, 98, 99, 100 (both), 101 (top right, bottom left and right), 102 (both), 103, 104 (both), 105, 106, 107 (both), 108 (both), 111

Illustrated London News Picture Library, pages 10, 11 (below)

Imperial War Museum, pages 12 (top), 13 (top)

National Portrait Gallery, London, pages 14, 15 (right), 54

Royal Collection, reproduced by gracious permission of Her Majesty Queen Elizabeth the Queen Mother, page 7